Diet recommendations during TCM - Stomach - Blood Stagnation

Please check these recommendations always with a nutrition consultant, therapist, doctor or dietician. The recipes and the list of ingredients are supporting the conventional medical therapy. The calorie disclosures of fresh ingredients (fruit and vegetables) vary according to quality and time of harvest. The contents were checked by a dietician and a nutrition consultant for the Traditional Chinese Medicine (TCM).

Author:
©2020 Josef Miligui
www.ebns.at

AF221624

Source:
The lists are created from the EBNS database for nutritional counseling. The database is used by dietitians, therapists and doctors for advising the patient / client.

Literature:
The specialist literature and the training documents of the German and Austrian dietary and traditional Chinese medicine serve as a knowledge base. We have used the documents as a basis of knowledge, adapted it to our experience and completed them.
http://nutribook.info/

Production and publishing:
BoD – Books on Demand, Norderstedt
ISBN: 9783752893953

(Book: E236)

Diet recommendations for TCM - Stomach - Blood Stagnation

1 Treatment strategy

Move stagnation, move blood (dissipate), lower stomach qi and harmonize stomach.

2 Avoid

n.a.

3 Breakfast

	kkal. per serving
Carrot and rice gruel soup	101
Celery juice	33
Cereal fruit pulp	175
Kuzu water	6
Oat flakes with aromatic spices	280
Rice congee with carrots and fennel -	131
Rice congee with crushed walnuts	406
Rice congee with honey pear and black sesame	158
Rice with parsnips	206
Tea from fennel	0
Tea from ground	2
Vegetable miso soup with tofu	106

4 Snack

Spring vegetables - also for babies from the 8th month 63

5 Lunch

Celery juice	33
Cereal fruit pulp	175
Kuzu water	6
Polenta with peach	197
Pumpkin soup	104
Rice congee with crushed walnuts	406
Rice congee with honey pear and black sesame	158
Rice with parsnips	206
Tea from anise	2,75

6 Afternoon

7 Dinner

8 Any time

9 Recipes

(rec.) = You can use more.
(little) = You should use less than specified
(omit) = omit.

9.1 Basic recipe for a reissue soup (Congee)

Warms the stomach and spleen, harmonizes the intestine, forces Qi, reduces moisture.
Cooking time approx. 2-4 hours
Calories p. portion: 140
3 portions

Quantity of ingredients
Rice variety any 1 cup / 120g. () - warm - sweet .... metal
Water 6 cups / 700g. (yes) - cool - salty .... earth

Cooking instructions:
Cook rice and water in a ratio of about 1: 6. The amount of water determines the thickness of the mash (matter of taste).
Put the rice in a saucepan with a heavy lid. It is important to simmer the rice after a short boil on the slightest flame, otherwise it burns.
Boil the rice for 2-4 hours. The longer he cooks, the more he strengthens.
If you want to eat the dish for breakfast, you can put the rice on just before bedtime.
To be on the safe side, you should first check the behavior of your pot and cooker under observation for a similar amount of time, so that nothing burns.
Refrigerate for later use.

9.2   Carrot and rice gruel soup

Warms the stomach and spleen, harmonizes the intestine, forces Qi, reduces moisture, strengthens spleen and liver, regulates Qi flow, moisturizes, relaxes, builds up Qi, spreads.
Cooking time approx. 10 min
Calories p. portion: 101
1 portions

Quantity of ingredients
Basic recipe for a rice soup (Congee) 1 cup / 120g. (rec.) - neutral - sweet..... *
Carrot 2 pieces / 100g. (rec.) - neutral - sweet..earth
Salt 1 teaspoon / 4g. (yes) - cold - salty ....water

Cooking instructions:
Peel and grate carrots. Heat the rice soup (according to the basic recipe) till it boils and add the grated carrots and salt. Cook for 10 minutes.

9.3   Celery juice

Strengthens stomach Qi, moisturizes, relaxes, builds up Qi, spreads.
Cooking time approx. 5 min
Calories p. portion: 33
1 portions
Allergens: L

Quantity of ingredients
Celery root 1/2 piece / 200g. (rec.) - cool - sweet.......................................earth
Water 1 cup / 120g. (yes) - cool - salty...earth
Salt 1 pinch / 0,5g. (yes) - cold - salty ....water

Cooking instructions:
Peel celeriac and cut into pieces and juice. Mix with water and salt as needed.

9.4   Cereal fruit pulp

Forces Qi.
Cooking time approx. 10 min
Calories p. portion: 175
1 portions
Allergens: A

Quantity of ingredients
Oat flakes (whole grain) 1/2 oz / 20g. (rec.) - warm - sweet......................metal
Water 3,5 oz / 90g. (yes) - cool - salty...earth
Apple juice (natural cloudy) 1/4 lbs - 4oz / 100g. (little) - cool - sweet........earth
Rapeseed oil 1/8 oz / 5g. (yes) - neutral - sweet...earth

Cooking instructions:
Heat the water till it boils the add the cereals. Instant flakes you only need to mix with hot water. Stir fruit juice or puree and grease. The fresh fruit (for example, apples, pears, peaches) can be raw or kneaded. Frozen fruit or industrially produced fruit jars without added sugar are also suitable. Bananas should be mixed with less sweet fruit.

9.5   Kuzu water

Moisturizes, relaxes, builds up Qi, spreads.
Cooking time approx. 5 min
Calories p. portion: 6
1 portions

Quantity of ingredients
Kuzu 1/2 teaspoon / 2g. (rec.) - hot - sweet ....earth
Water 1 cup / 120g. (yes) - cool - salty...earth

Cooking instructions:
Pound Kuzu, pour in lukewarm water and let steep until a milky liquid is formed. Then strain.

9.6 Oat flakes with aromatic spices

Nourishes fluids, reduces stomach heat, forces spleen, produces essence, harmonizes stomach, forces Qi, strengthens kidney Qi, essence and brain, moisturizes, relaxes, spreads.
Cooking time approx. 25 min
Calories p. portion: 280
3 portions
Allergens: AH

Quantity of ingredients
Oat flakes (whole grain) 1 cup / 125g. (rec.) - warm - sweet .... metal
Walnuts 1 table spoon / 15g. (yes) - warm - sweet .... earth
Hazelnuts 1 table spoon / 15g. (yes) - neutral - sweet .... earth
Water 1 1/2 cups / 240g. (yes) - cool - salty .... earth
Wakame 1 inch / 2g. () - cold - salty .... water
Apple (sweet) 1 piece / 220g. (little) - cool - sweet, sour .... earth
Cardamom 3-4 capsules / 2g. () - warm - acrid .... *
Lemon Balm (fresh) 3-4 leaves / 3g. () - cool - sour .... metal
Acerola fruit nectar or powder 1 teaspoon / 2g. () - warm - sour .... wood

Cooking instructions:
Roast oatmeal and nuts. Add hot water. Add cardamom, wakame and cook for 20 min. Add grated apple, acerola and lemon herb.

9.7 Polenta with peach

Strengthens blood and fluids, brings blood into motion, builds up Qi, spreads, strengthens stomach Qi, diuretic, moisturizes, relaxes, builds up Qi, spreads, warms the stomach and spleen, promotes blood circulation and conduction flow, relieves colds.
Cooking time approx. 20 min
Calories p. portion: 197
3 portions

Quantity of ingredients
Water 1 1/2 cups / 240g. (yes) - cool - salty .... earth
Corn Grease (Polenta) 1 cup / 120g. (rec.) - neutral - sweet .... earth
Peaches 2-3 pieces / 400g. (yes) - warm - sour, sweet .... earth
Vanilla pod 1 pinch / 1g. () - neutral - sweet .... *
Chili (pod or ground) 1 pinch / 0,1g. (little) - hot - acrid .... metal
Cinnamon ground 1 pinch / 1g. (little) - hot - acrid, sweet .... *

Cooking instructions:
Pour the polenta into a pan of hot water with constant stirring until the polenta has the desired consistency. Pull the polenta from the fire and let it soak for 10 minutes.

Wash fresh peaches and cut into quarters. Pour into the finished polenta the peaches, add the vanilla and add Chili to taste, stir and let it go for 3 minutes.

Winter varieties: Pickled fruit, pear, apples

9.8 Pumpkin soup

Forces lungs and spleen, diuretic, forces Qi, protects liver, forces Qi, forces spleen, relieves inflammation, moisturizes, relaxes, builds up Qi, spreads, strengthens spleen and liver, regulates Qi flow, moisturizes, relaxes, builds up Qi, spreads.
Cooking time approx. 1 hour
Calories p. portion: 105
3 portions

Quantity of ingredients
Pumpkin 3/4 lbs / 300g. (rec.) - warm - sweet.............................earth
Carrot 2 pieces / 100g. (rec.) - neutral - sweet...........................earth
Potato 2 pieces / 120g. (yes) - neutral - sweet............................earth
Olive oil 1 table spoon / 10g. (little) - cool - sweet.....................earth
Onion white 1 piece / 50g. (little) - warm - acrid ....metal
Water 1 cup / 120g. (yes) - cool - salty......................................earth
Parsley 1 table spoon / 7g. (yes) - warm - bitter.......................... wood
Anise (Common Fennel) 1 pinch / 1g. (rec.) - warm - acrid.......................earth
Salt 1 pinch / 1g. (yes) - cold - salty .... water

Cooking instructions:
Add the olive oil to the pan, add the diced pumpkin, diced carrots and potatoes. Roast them shortly, add the finely chopped onion, fill with water, add enough water to cover the vegetables at least 3 finger-widths. Boil at low heat.

Season with sea salt, add small cutted parsley, a pinch of anise (little). Allow to simmer for about 35 minutes. Then purée the soup and add some water, depending on the consistency of the soup.

9.9 Rice congee with carrots and fennel

Nutritious builds up Qi, forces the digestive functions.
Cooking time approx. 2 hours and more
Calories p. portion: 131
3 portions
Allergens: G

Quantity of ingredients
Basic recipe for a rice soup (Congee) 2 cup / 500g. (rec.) - neutral - sweet..... *
Carrot 2 pieces / 100g. (rec.) - neutral - sweet...earth
Fennel 1 piece / 250g. (rec.) - warm - sweet, little acrid.............................earth
Butter organic 1 teaspoon / 3g. (yes) - neutral - sweet...............................earth
Cardamom 1/2 teaspoon / 1g. () - warm - acrid.. *

Cooking instructions:
Cook rice congee according to basic recipe.
Clean and cut carrots and fennel.

When carrots and fennel are cooked from the beginning, they serve wholesomeness. If added shortly before the end of the cooking time, taste and vitamins are retained.

Refine with butter and cardamom before serving.

9.10 Rice congee with crushed walnuts

Nourishing and slightly warming, warms the middle, builds up Qi, warms the stomach and spleen, harmonizes the intestine, forces Qi, reduces moisture.
Cooking time approx. 2 hours and more
Calories p. portion: 406
2 portions
Allergens: H

Quantity of ingredients
Basic recipe for a rice soup (Congee) 4 cups / 500g. (rec.) - neutral - sweet... *
Sugar cane sugar 2 table spoons / 20g. (little) - cool - sweet....................earth
Walnuts 1 cup / 70g. (yes) - warm - sweet ....earth
Cinnamon ground 1 pinch / 0,2g. (little) - hot - acrid, sweet .... *

Cooking instructions:
Cook the basic recipe for rice soup (congee)
Note: The crushed walnuts can be cooked from the beginning.

Variation: Refine with sweet or spicy ingredients as you like. In particular, cinnamon, cloves, and ginger increase the warming effect and wholesomeness.

9.11 Rice congee with honey pear and black sesame

Especially good in kidney Yin deficiency, moisturizes lungs, cools heat, reduces lung mucus, produces humors, moisturizes, relaxes, builds up Qi, spreads, moisturizes intestines, nourishes Yin.
Cooking time approx. 10 min - 3 hours
Calories p. portion: 158
2 portions
Allergens: N

Quantity of ingredients
Basic recipe for a rice soup (Congee) 1 1/2 cups / 240g. (rec.) - neutral - sweet
*
Pear 2 pieces / 300g. (little) - cool - sweet, sour ....earth

Cooking instructions:
Cook rice congee according to basic recipe.
Fill pot with 3 cm of water and heat till it boils. Quarter the pears (with the skin and seeds) and simmer them covered with black sesame for 10 minutes. Mix with the rice.

9.12 Rice with parsnips

Regulates Qi, dries out, passes downwardly, warms the stomach and spleen, harmonizes the intestine, forces Qi, reduces moisture. moisturizes, relaxes, builds up Qi, spreads. distributes mucus, activates Wei Qi, forces Qi.
Cooking time approx. 45 min
Calories p. portion: 206
3 portions

Quantity of ingredients
Rice variety any 1 cup / 120g. () - warm - sweet ....metal
Water 1 1/2 cups / 200g. (yes) - cool - salty ....earth
Salt 1 pinch / 1g. (yes) - cold - salty ....water
Parsnip 3-4 pieces / 450g. (rec.) - cool - bitter ....fire
Olive oil 1 table spoon / 10g. (little) - cool - sweet......................................earth
Sage 1 teaspoon / 3g. (little) - neutral - bitter, spicy ....fire

Cooking instructions:
Peel the parsnips and cut into slices. Fry for a short time in oil. Add the rice and fry again for a short time. Add the water and cook it at least 30 min. Sprinkle with fresh chopped sage.

9.13 Spring vegetables

Cools heat, diuretic, cools blood, reduces mucus, moisturizes, relaxes, builds Qi, distributes, strengthen the middle, nourishes lung Yin, produces humors.
Cooking time approx. 1 1/2 hour
Calories p. portion: 64
8 portions
Allergens: G

Quantity of ingredients
Carrot 1,1 lbs / 500g. (rec.) - neutral - sweet...earth
Kohlrabi 1,1 lbs / 500g. (yes) - neutral - acrid, sweet ....earth
Butter organic 2 table spoons / 20g. (yes) - neutral - sweet.......................earth
Water 1/2 cup / 125g. (yes) - cool - salty...earth

Cooking instructions:
Wash the vegetables thoroughly. Clean and peel carrots and turnip cabbage. From the turnip cabbage, finely chop some delicate leaves and set aside. Rasp the carrots and the turnip cabbage. Melt the butter, add the water and the vegetables and cook over medium heat for about 30 minutes. Stir occasionally. Spread the vegetables and cooked water to about 8 deep-frozen bags to a100-150 g (depending on the age of the child). Close the bags, allow them to cool down and freeze them for max 3 months.
If necessary, thaw, boil and mix with 80g of boiled potatoes and an egg. (The recipe can easily be varied if you want to use cauliflower, peas or zucchini)

9.14 Tea from anise

Warms the middle, forces stomach and spleen, warms stomach, reduces cold-evil, harmonizes stomach-Qi, warms kidney.
Cooking time approx. 15 min
Calories p. portion: 3
4 portions

Quantity of ingredients

Anise (Common Fennel) 1 teaspoon / 3g. (rec.) - warm - acrid..................earth
Water 2 cup / 500g. (yes) - cool - salty..earth

Cooking instructions:

Heat the water till it boils and put it aside. Add anise.
10 min. to let go.
Pour through a tea strainer. Sweet to taste with honey.

In order to achieve a salutary effect, you should drink 2 cups of anise
tea per day.

9.15 Tea from fennel

Forces Yang, reduces cold-evil, harmonizes stomach-Qi.
Cooking time approx. 10 min
Calories p. portion: 0
4 portions

Quantity of ingredients

Fennel tea 2 table spoons / 20g. (rec.) - warm - acrid................................earth
Water 2 cup / 500g. (yes) - cool - salty..earth

Cooking instructions:

Heat the water till it boils and put it aside. Add fennel tea and 10 min. to
let go. Sweet to taste with honey. Strain when pouring.
Tea from ground
Reduces mucus and moist heat in the liver and gallbladder, against liver
Qi stagnation, spleen qi deficiency, spleen and kidney Yang- deficiency.
Cooking time approx. 10 min
Calories p. portion: 2
4 portions

Quantity of ingredients

Ground 1 teaspoon / 3g. (rec.) - warm - acrid ....metal
Water 2 cup / 500g. (yes) - cool - salty..earth

Cooking instructions:

Heat the water till it boils and put it aside. Add crushed cumin and leave
for 10 min. to let go. Sweet to taste with honey. Strain when pouring.

Drink 1 cup 2 times a day.

9.16 Tea from rose hip

Strengthens spleen Qi.
Cooking time approx. 10 min
Calories p. portion: 2
4 portions

Quantity of ingredients
Rose hip tea 2 table spoons / 4g. (yes) - warm - sour, sweet................... wood
Water 2 cup / 500g. (yes) - cool - salty...earth

Cooking instructions:
Heat the water till it boils and put it aside. Add rosehip and leave for 10 min. to let go. Sweet to taste with honey. Strain when pouring.

9.17 Tender fennel vegetables

Regulates Qi, warms the inside, lowers cold, forces stomach, relieves constipation, forces Yang, dissolves mucus, reduces wind, spreads.
Cooking time approx. 25 min
Calories p. portion: 70
2 portions
Allergens: G

Quantity of ingredients
Potato 1 piece / 50g. (yes) - neutral - sweet...earth
Fennel 1/4 lbs - 4oz / 100g. (rec.) - warm - sweet, little acrid....................earth
Water 2 table spoons / 20g. (yes) - cool - salty ....earth
Butter organic 1 table spoon / 10g. (yes) - neutral - sweet........................earth

Cooking instructions:
Wash the potato and peel with a peeler. Cut into cubes of about 2 cm. Wash the fennel, remove stained, dark spots and cut the tuber. Heat till it boils with 2 tablespoons of water in a small saucepan. Cook on low heat for about 15 minutes. Fish out the caraway seeds. Puree the vegetables with the blender and stir in the butter.
Fennel and caraway soothe the stomach and prevent bloating. In addition, fennel contains a lot of vitamin C and folic acid. An ideal meal for sick children.

9.18 Vegetable miso soup with tofu

Strengthens spleen and liver, regulates Qi flow, moisturizes, relaxes, builds up Qi, spreads, forces Qi, forces liver and kidney, reduces damp heat, detoxifies, nourishes fluids, reduces internal heat, dries out, passes downwardly.
Cooking time approx. 15 min
Calories p. portion: 107
4 portions
Allergens: EN

Quantity of ingredients
Sesame oil 2 table spoons / 35g. (little) - cool - sweet ....earth
Onion (shallot) 1 piece / 20g. (little) - warm - acrid, sweet........................metal
Carrot 1 piece / 70g. (rec.) - neutral - sweet..earth
Leek 2 inches / 10g. (little) - warm - acrid..metal
Water 3 cups / 750g. (yes) - cool - salty..earth
Endive salad 2 table spoons / 30g. () - neutral - bitter...................................fire
Soy Tofu 2 table spoons / 30g. (rec.) - cool - sweet...................................earth
Ginger fresh 1/2 teaspoon / 1g. (rec.) - warm - acrid...............................metal
Miso 2 table spoons / 15g. (rec.) - neutral - salty ....water

Cooking instructions:
In sesame oil first sauté onions, then carrots and a little leek; Pour in water and simmer gently; add the bean sprouts and endive leaves and leave to stand; Tofu cubes, add a little ginger; at the end stir in a little cooled cooking-water the Miso.

10 Effects of food

10.1 Use ingredients: recommendable

Anise (Common Fennel)
Basic recipe for a fish soup
Basic recipe for a rice soup (Congee)
Black caraway
Carrot
Carrot (Early Carrot)
Carrot juice without sugar
Celery root
Coriander
Corn Grease (Polenta)
Fennel
Fennel tea
Ginger fresh
Gourd
Ground

Ground caraway
Miso
Oat flakes (whole grain)
Oat fusion (baby food)
Parsley root
Parsnip
Pumpkin
Rice Basmati
Soy Tofu
Spelled semolina
Sweet potato
Thyme
Turnips
Umeboshi plums (Japanese apricots)
Vanilla

10.2 Use ingredients: yes

Amaranth
Apricots
Arrowroot
Basil
Basil (fresh)
Bitter melon
Black tea
Black-eyed peas
Boxhorn clover seeds
Breadcrumbs (wheat bread, bread roll)
Butter organic
Carp
Celery sticks
Chervil
Chestnuts
Chicken egg
Clove
Coconut flakes
Cod
Couscous
Cumin (Caraway seed)
Dates dried
Dill
Fig
Fig dried
Fish pieces mixed (fresh water)
French beans
Goose

Goose parts
Grass carp
Hawthorn
Hazelnuts
Herbs various
Hyssop
Juniper berry
Kohlrabi
Kumquats
Lentils
Lentils black
Lentils red
Lentils yellow
Lovage
Marjoram
Mediterranean fish (cod, plaice, haddock, sea eel, mackerel)
Morel (black, dried)
Multi-grain bread (gray bread)
Mustard seeds
Oat flour
Octopus
Okra
Oregano dried
Papaya
Parsley
Peaches
Peaches (canned)

Peanut oil
Peas
Peppers
Peppers (rose peppers)
Perch
Pheasant
Pine nuts
Pistachios
Plaice
Poppy
Potato
Pumpkin seed oil
Pumpkin seeds
Quinoa
Radish black
Rapeseed oil
Rose hip tea
Rosemary
Sake

Salmon
Salt
Savory
Sesame paste (Tahini)
Sour milk cheese 20%
Soybean oil
Soybeans, black
Soybeans, yellow
Spiny lobsters
Star anise
Sunflower seeds
Turmeric (yellow root)
Vanilla powder
Walnuts
Water
Water hot
Wheat semolina
Wheat semolina for children
White bread (wheat bread)

10.3 Use ingredients: little

Adzuki beans
Apple (sour)
Apple (sweet)
Apple juice (natural cloudy)
Apricot
Artichoke
Aubergine
Balm
Barley
Beer (Pils)
Beer (Top-fermented German dark beer)
Broccoli
Brussels sprouts
Buckwheat
Bulgur (cereals)
Buttermilk
Calamari
Cashews
Cauliflower
Cereal coffee
Chard
Cherry
Cherry juice
Chicken meat
Chickpeas
Chili (pod or ground)
Chinese cabbage
Chives
Cinnamon ground
Cinnamon sticks
Clementines

Cocoa
Coconut grated
Coconut milk
Coffee
Coix (seeds) YiYi Ren
Cow's milk (1.5% fat)
Cow's milk (whole milk 3.5% fat)
Cream, sweet 30%
Cress
Curcuma
Curd cheese 20%
Curd cheese 40%
Deer meat
Deer meat
Duck (heart)
Duck (slaughtered)
Elderberry blossom tee
Feta cheese
Fresh cheese
Ginger powder
Goat
Goat and sheep's milk
Goat cheese
Grapes red
Lamb bones
Lamb meat
Leek
Lemon peel
Longane
Lychee
Lychee in Preserved
Margarine

Margarine (diet)
Millet
Millet flakes
Mozzarella
Oat
Olive oil
Olives
Onion (shallot)
Onion (spring onion)
Onion read
Onion white
Oysters
Parmesan
Peanuts
Pear
Pear juice
Peas, green
Pepper white (ground)
Pomegranate
Pork skin
Quail
Quail egg
Quince
Rabbit meat
Raisins
Red cabbage

Rye
Rye flour
Sage
Salsify
Savoy cabbage / kale
Sesame oil
Soybean milk
Spelled (Dark) bread
Spelled grain
Spelled wholemeal flour
Spinach
Sugar brown
Sugar candy white
Sugar cane sugar
Sugar fructose - fruit sugar
Sugar glucose - grapes sugar
Sugar Milk Sugar
Sunflower oil
Tarragon (Estragon)
Turkey breast meat
Vegetable juice
Wheat flour
Wheat germ oil
White cabbage
Wild boar meat
Zucchini

10.4 Do not use contra-acting foods

Agar agar (kelp)
Asparagus (green or white)
Avocado
Bamboo shoots
Banana
Banana (cooking banana)
Boletus mushroom
Burdock root tea
Carambola (Star fruit)
Champignon
Chanterelle
Crab
Cranberry
Cranberry juice
Cucumber
Currant (black)
Currant (red)
Currant (white)
Curry
Dandelionroots tea
Garlic
Gooseberry
Grapefruit (Pomelo)
Grapefruit juice
Kefir

Kiwi
Lemon
Lemon juice
Lime
Mallow (Malva sylvestris) blossom tea
Mango
Mineral water
Miso paste (soy bean paste)
Mold cheese
Morel, dried
Mulberry fruit
Mullet
Mussels
Mutton
Nutmeg
Orange
Orange juice
Oyster mushroom
Pepper Cayenne
Peppercorns
Pickle
Pimento
Pineapple
Pineapple (from a can)
Pineapple juice without sugar

Plum
Pork meat
Rabbit liver
Radish
Radish (white, green, purple-red)
Reishi mushroom
Rhubarb
Sauerkraut (cutted cabbage fermented)
Seacrab
Shiitake, dried
Sorrel
Sour cherries
Sour cream 15% fat
Sour milk
Soy sauce

Spirit
Strawberries
Strawberry Juice
Sugar white
Tangerine
Tomato
Vinegar (Apple vinegar)
Vinegar (Red wine vinegar)
Vinegar Aceto Balsamico
Watermelon
Wild strawberries
Yarrow tea
Yogi tea
Yogurt (natural, 1.5% fat)
Yogurt (natural, 3.5% fat)

11 Complementary

11.1 Pepper (black)

Piperis nigri, Fructus
Preparation: Decoction
Reduces internal heat and moisture, reduces wind-coldness, promotes Qi-flow. To balance the cold yin energy, salads made from fresh raw vegetables can be seasoned generously with black pepper, the hot yang herb.
1.5-3 g, drink in two doses 30-40 minutes after eating
Do not use in case of: Inflammation in the digestive tract.

12 Basics of Nutrition

The basic principles of nutrition described herein are general recommendations. They are not aimed at a specific form of therapy. Recommendations concerning a therapy have priority.

12.1 Nutrition

Regular meals in a relaxed atmosphere. A warm breakfast is considered a good start into the day.
The main meals ought to be taken for lunch – supper in the early evening. Pay attention to feeling hungry or sated: don't eat too much nor remain hungry is the rule
Prepare the meals freshly from natural, regional products. Frozen, heat-conserved, industrially prepared or foodstuffs cooked in the microwave oven are rejected.
Choice of foodstuffs according to the season: more cooling food in summer, more warming food in winter.
Eat cooked food at least twice a day. Food and drinks ought to be lukewarm, never ice-cold or hot.
Raw vegetables, briefly cooked vegetables, freshly squeezed juices and mineral water are not recommended. Milk and dairy products are only included in the diet if they don't cause problems. Don't use therapeutic recipes over a longer period without consulting your doctor or therapist.

Varied food
Enjoy the diversity of foodstuffs. Characteristics of a balanced nutrition are variety, suitable combination and a balanced quantity of rich and low energy foodstuffs (on one hand avoiding undersupply with essential nutrients and on the other hand to take to many undesirable substances).

A lot of Cereal Products - and Potatoes
Bread, pasta, rice, cereal flakes (best wholemeal) as well as potatoes contain almost no fat, but many vitamins, mineral nutrients, trace elements, roughage and secondary plant substances. These foodstuffs ought to be taken with low-fat side dishes.

Vegetables and Fruit – „Take Five" every day … 5 portions of vegetables and fruit a day, as fresh as possible, briefly cooked, or maybe one portion as a juice – ideal as a side dish to every meal as well as snack between meals: Thus a lot of vitamins, mineral nutrients as well as roughage and secondary plant substances

Daily milk and dairy products
Milk and Dairy Products every Day, once or twice per Week Fish; meat, sausages as well as eggs moderately. These foodstuffs contain valuable nutrients like calcium in the milk, iodine selenium and omega-3 fat acids in saltwater fish. Meat is favorable due to its high content of disposable iron and the vitamins B1, B6 and B12. Quantities of 300 – 600 g meat and sausage per week are sufficient. Prefer low-fat products, especially in meat- and dairy products.

Low-fat and fatty Foodstuffs
Fat supplies us with essential fat acids and fatty foodstuffs contain also fat-soluble vitamins. Fat is high in energy; therefore much fat in the food may cause overweight, possibly also cancer. Too many saturated fat acids may further a tendency for cardio-vascular diseases in the long term. Prefer vegetable oils and fats (e.g. rapeseed-, olive-, soya-oils and solid fats produced therefrom). Beware of invisible fat in meat- and dairy products, pastry and sweets as well as in fast-food and convenience foods. 70 – 90 g fat per day is sufficient.

Moderately Sugar and Salt
Take sugar and foods/drinks containing various kinds of sugar (e.g. glucose syrup) only occasionally. Use herbs and spices as well as a little salt creatively. Prefer salt containing iodine.

Plenty of Liquids
Water is absolutely essential. Drink 1-2 l liquids every day. Prefer water (with or without gas) and other low-calorie drinks. Alcoholic drinks should not be taken.

Tasty Dishes, carefully cooked
Cook the meals with as low temperatures and as short as possible, using little water and fat – this preserves the original taste, keeps the nutrients intact and prevents the production of harmful compounds.

Take time and enjoy the food
Take your Time and enjoy your Food
Eating consciously helps to eat right. The eye enjoys food, too. It's fun, invites to enjoy varied dishes and stimulates the feeling of satiety.

Watch your Weight and stay in Motion
A balanced diet and a lot of exercise and sport (30 – 60 min/day) are a healthy combination. The right weight furthers well-being and health.

Thermals, directional effectiveness, digestive power
There are various criteria for judging the effectiveness of herbs and foodstuffs.

The use of certain herbs and ingredients is based on observations of the effects on the body which these foodstuffs, herbs and spices show after having eaten them. The medical science has developed following system: Every ingredient or herb has a directional effectiveness. Furthermore, there are herbs which have a special effect on certain organs.

The basic condition for a healthy metabolism is to obtain sufficient energy from food and that the digestive process doesn't use too much energy. An easily digestible meal makes content and sated, doesn't cause flatulence and fatigue after the meal. The perfect spices increase the healthiness of our meals. Very often, just small doses of herbs and spices will suffice. They are not used to make us sated, but to help our digestive organs to digest the food.

12.2 Recipes

The recipes list the ingredients to be used and the cooking instructions show how the dish is prepared. The list of ingredients shows the concerned quantities as well as the relevance for the therapy. If you find „omit", try to comply or find an alternative from the „list of recommended foodstuffs". Mostly it shall result just in a small change of taste when you simply avoid this ingredient.

Mild cooking methods: boiling, stewing, poaching, steaming
Strong cooking methods: barbecuing, roasting, frying, smoking
Balanced cooking methods: deep-frying, baking brick
Deep-freezing and warming in the microwave oven should be avoided (denaturalization).

12.3 Foodstuffs

Foodstuffs have an effect on body and soul like medicinal herbs, only a very much milder one. Dietary advice is mainly based on regional foodstuffs. The knowledge about the effects of each foodstuff and the knowledge, when which foodstuff shall be used, is based on the school medicine. Use ecologic-organic products, if possible. As everything should be cooked for a long time due to a better digestability and very rarely eaten raw, the food agrees with everyone.

The classification of the foodstuffs according to their effect on the body is the basis in order to achieve a harmonious status of health.

Dietary advisors do not recommend certain foodstuffs for everyone. The individual diet is tailor-made for the individual constitution.

Buy only fresh and ripe fruit and vegetables. You ought to leave unripe fruit and vegetables and such with brown spots and wilted leaves behind in the market. In this case take deep-frozen goods (never ready-to-serve dishes!). Fruit and vegetables are deep-frozen immediately after harvesting and often contain more vitamins and minerals than the goods from the vegetable shelf. Whereas conserved or tinned goods contain very much less biological substances. Also, salt, sugar and others are mostly added to the latter. Never leave the foodstuffs in the water after washing them to avoid that many vital substances get drowned. Clean salads, fruit and vegetables immediately before serving.

Please make sure of the hygienic processing of foodstuffs. Clean your salads, fruit and vegetables carefully. When cooking with meat, prepare all ingredients first and then process the meat products. Clean the worktop and tools very carefully. Wooden surfaces ought to be treated with a mild disinfectant regularly in order to reduce germination. Store fruit and vegetables separately, if possible. Harvested fruit and vegetables are still alive and emit e.g. ethylene gas, which makes other products ripen and age faster. Keep meat and fish in the closed packaging or store them in the fridge in closed containers.

12.4 Herbs

There are some basic rules for storing medicinal herbs. On principle, herbs must be protected from direct sunlight, humidity and heat.

Containers for the storage of herbs may be glasses, ceramic jars and even plastic containers. However, plastic is a rather unsuitable material and should only be a short-term solution. In case of glass containers, use a dark material.

Medicinal herbs cannot be kept for any long period. The shelf life of herbs is limited. However, it can be prolonged with suitable storage. The place should be dark, rather cool and absolutely dry. A wooden medicine cabinet, placed not directly next to a source of heat, would be ideal. Never buy large quantities of herbs so as not to have to throw them away. Label the container with the name of the herb and the date of harvesting or processing.

13 Other dietic-books

The following syndromes of dietetics, TCM or for a therapy supplement for cancer are available.

Dietetics

E001. Nutrition of the infant - baby food
E002. Nutrition during lactation
E003. Nutrition in old age
E004. Nutrition of children and adolescents
E005. Nutrition of athletes
E006. Light weight
E007. Pregnancy
E008. Full food

Protein and electrolyte - kidneys
E009. (hemodialysis) dialysis treatment
E010. Acute renal failure
E011. Chronic renal insufficiency
E012. Nephrotic syndrome
E013. Kidney stones (nephrolithiasis)

Gastrointestinal tract - pancreas
E014. Acute pancreatitis (inflammation of the pancreas)
E015. Chronic pancreatitis (inflammation of the pancreas)

Gastrointestinal tract - small intestine and large intestine
E016. Acute obstipation (constipation)
E017. Chronic obstipation (constipation)
E018. Colon irritabile
E019. Diverticulitis
E020. Acquired lactose intolerance (lactose malabsorption)
E021. Fructose malabsorption
E022. Glutensensitive enteropathy (celiac disease)
E023. Colectomy
E024. Short Bowel Syndrome

Gastrointestinal tract - liver, gallbladder, bile ducts
E025. Acute and chronic hepatitis (inflammation of the liver)
E026. Cholelithiasis (bile stones)
E027. fatty liver
E028. cirrhosis

Gastrointestinal tract - Stomach and duodenal intestine
E029. Acute gastritis
E030. Chronic gastritis
E031. Stomach bleeding
E032. Ulcus ventriculi and duodenal ulcer
E033. Condition after gastric surgery

Gastrointestinal tract - oral cavity and esophagus
E034. Stomatitis
E035. Esophageal carcinoma (esophageal cancer)
E036. Refluosophagitis (heartburn)

Special diseases
E037. Phenylketonuria (PKU)
E038. Rheumatic joint diseases

Metabolism
E039. Obesity (overweight)
E040. Diabetes mellitus
E041. Eating disorders (underweight)

Fat metabolism
E042. Hypercholesterolaemia (increased cholesterol level)
E043. Hepatic Encephalopathy

Heart and circulation
E044. Arteriosclerosis (arterial calcification)
E045. Heart insufficiency
E046. Hypertension
E047. Hyperuricaemia and gout

Changed nutrient requirements
E048. In case of fever
E049. For malignant diseases
E050. After burns
E051. Radiation and chemotherapy

CANCER
E100. Pancreatic cancer
E101. Bladder cancer
E102. Blood cancer (leukemia)
E103. Breast cancer
E104. Colorectal cancer
E105. Gastric cancer
E106. Kidney cancer
E107. Esophageal cancer

TCM
E200. Bladder - moisture heat in the bladder
E201. Bladder - moisture and cold in the bladder
E202. Bladder - emptiness and cold in the bladder
E203. Large intestine - external cold affects the large intestine
E204. Large intestine - moisture heat in the large intestine
E205. Large intestine - heat blocks the intestine II acute
E206. Large intestine - dryness of the colon
E207. Large intestine - Yang deficiency (cold)
E208. Heart - Blood insufficiency
E209. Heart - Blood stagnation
E210. Heart - Fire
E211. Heart - Hot mucus clogs the heart pores

E212. Heart - Cold mucus clogs the heart pores
E213. Heart - Qi deficiency
E214. Heart - Yang deficiency
E215. Heart - Yin deficiency
E216. Liver - Ascending Liver Yang
E217. Liver - Blood deficiency
E218. Liver - Blood stagnation
E219. Liver - Moisture heat in liver and gall bladder
E220. Liver - Fire
E221. Liver - Gall bladder Qi-Empty
E222. Liver - Cold in the liver meridian
E223. Liver - Qi stagnation
E224. Liver - Wind
E225. Liver - Wind with ascending liver Yang
E226. Liver - Wind with blood anemic
E227. Liver - Wind with extreme heat
E228. Lung - Qi deficiency
E229. Lung - Mucus-moisture in the lungs
E230. Lung - Mucus-heat in the lungs
E231. Lung - Mucus-cold in the lungs
E232. Lung - Dryness of the lungs
E233. Lung - Wind-heat attacks the lungs
E234. Lung - Wind-cold affects the lungs
E235. Lung - Yin deficiency
E236. Stomach - Bloodstagnation
E237. Stomach - Fire
E238. Stomach - Cold with liquid
E239. Stomach - Nutrition stagnation
E240. Stomach - Qi deficiency
E241. Stomach - Rebellious Qi
E242. Stomach - Yin Emptiness
E243. Spleen - Heat and moisture attack the spleen
E244. Spleen - Coldness and moisture affects the spleen
E245. Spleen - Qi deficiency
E246. Spleen - Qi deficiency + Declining spleen Qi
E247. Spleen - Qi deficiency + spleen does not control the blood
E248. Spleen - Yang deficiency
E249. Kidney - Heart and kidney no longer communicate
E250. Kidney - Jing deficiency
E251. Kidney - Kidneys cannot receive the Qi
E252. Kidney - Qi is not stable
E253. Kidney - Yang deficiency
E254. Kidney - Yin deficiency

For further information visit nutribook.info.

14 EBNS - Software for nutritional counseling

The main task of the database is to create personalized nutritional advice for each patient individually. The database was developed for Dietetics and Traditional Chinese Medicine.

The Database supports training and advices in the daily work routine.

The computer program provides lists of recipes, ingredients and herbs, which are given to the client. individually adjustable according to patient's request from whole food to vegetarians (lacto, ovo, ...). For every register there is an information sheet which can be given to the client. All texts can be individually designed.

The syndromes can be combined and result in an intersection of the recommended recipes and ingredients. The automated diagnosis for the TCM enables you to check your experience during the training as well as to confirm your diagnosis in the working day. You select several predefined symptoms and have the program automatically display the relevant syndromes.

How to work with the database:
Select the patient / client, select one or more of the syndromes you diagnosed and print the folder.

You can change all values, create new symptoms or syndromes, develop recipes, change or adapt ingredients and herbs to your findings. In simple client management, all relevant data about the person is stored. You get an overview of the past diagnoses and the development of the course of the disease.

As a consultant you save a lot of time when you print out the recipe, food and herbal lists for the recognized syndromes and give them to the clients. You can use this time for a personal conversation. With the database, dieticians and nutritionists can view the nutrients and trace elements for each recipe and develop recipes for syndromes even with suggested ingredients.

All recipe and grocery lists can also be ordered from me as a combination of several diseases. I wish all readers good luck, health and happiness in life.
More information can be found at www.ebns.at.
Volunteer: www.krebsinfo.at
Josef Miligui